To Azra Naz (my ♡ my sister!)

Happy Laughs!

I Froze My Mother
and Other Seriously Funny Family Poems

3/4

I Froze My Mother

and Other Seriously Funny Family Poems

poems by Ted Scheu

photographs by Peter Lourie

Young Poets' Press

MIDDLEBURY, VT

I Froze My Mother
Second Edition, December 2009

Text copyright © 2005 by Ted Scheu
Photographs copyright © 2005 by Peter Lourie
Design by Winslow Colwell/WColwell Design

Published in the United States by Young Poets' Press
PO Box 564, Middlebury, VT 05753
www.youngpoetspress.com

Grateful acknowledgement is made to the publishers of the following publications in which work previously appeared:

   "Sleep Tricks" originally appeared in the anthology: *If Kids Ruled the School,* 2004, Meadowbrook Press.

   "My Pain" and "The Man Who Named the Funny Bone" originally appeared in the anthology: *The Poetry Store,* 2005, Hodder Children's Books, UK.

The text of this publication was set in American Typewriter.

ISBN 978-0-9825499-1-9
Library of Congress Control Number: 2007937697

To Robin, Jamie & Kirsten

With love & thanks

Table of Contents

I'm Gonna Be My Best Today

I'm gonna be my best today
in everything I do.
For all to see, I aim to be
a parent's dream come true.

I'll always pay attention
and listen extra clearly.
I'll do my chores when I am asked—
well... sorta, kinda, nearly.

At meals, I'll try my utmost
not to burp or spill.
And after that I'll brush my teeth—
at least I hope I will.

The words I speak will be polite
and not unkind or gross.
I may not be a perfect kid
but I'll be pretty close.

I'm gonna be my best today—
a superstar, and then,
when tomorrow rolls around
I'll be myself again.

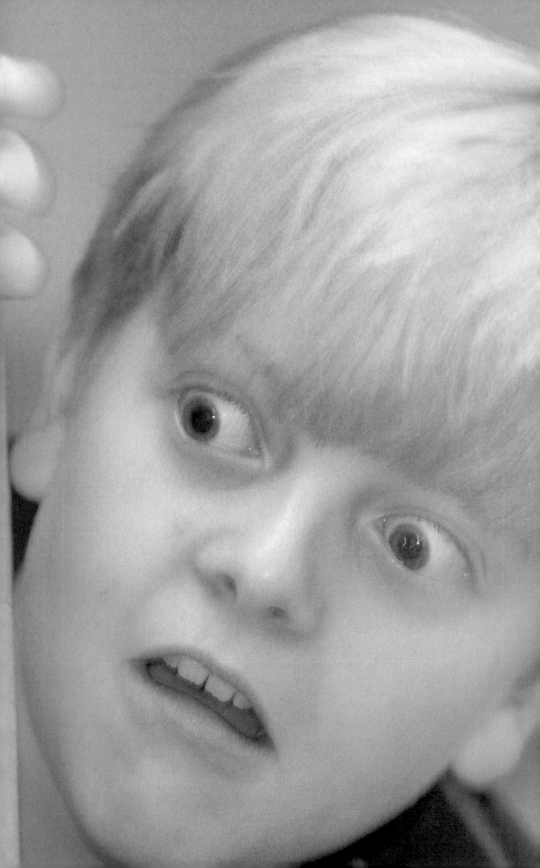

The Alien in Our Bathroom

There's an alien in our bathroom
with a white and wild face.
His belly's big, his legs are thin.
He looks like he just staggered in
from deepest outer space.

He grabbed at me with drippy claws
as I walked past the door.
I'm lucky he was out of shape.
I kicked and screamed and just escaped
by diving to the floor.

It's much too early in my day
for monsters misbehaving.
I think I'll hide, completely still,
and wait and listen here until
the alien's finished shaving.

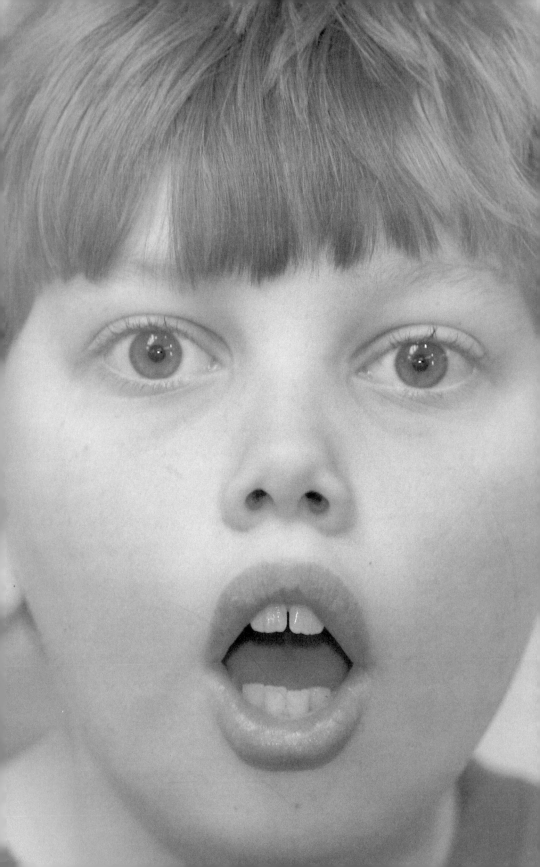

I Froze My Mother

Yesterday the strangest thing
I've ever seen occurred.
I froze my mother in her tracks
with just a single word.

Her arms went limp, her eyes got wide,
her fork fell on the floor.
I've never seen my Mom
exactly act that way before.

I got a little scared at first
and kept my fingers crossed.
But when she blinked and laughed
I knew she'd started to defrost.

I'll never know for certain
what made her freak and freeze.
She asked me if I wanted more
and all I said was "Please."

And then, today, she made my lunch
I told her "Thanks!" and then,
my very silly mother went
and froze right up again.

I Got a New Dog

I got a new dog
for my brother today.
I told her to "sit"
and she stayed.

I got a new dog
for my brother today.
I think it was
a pretty good trade.

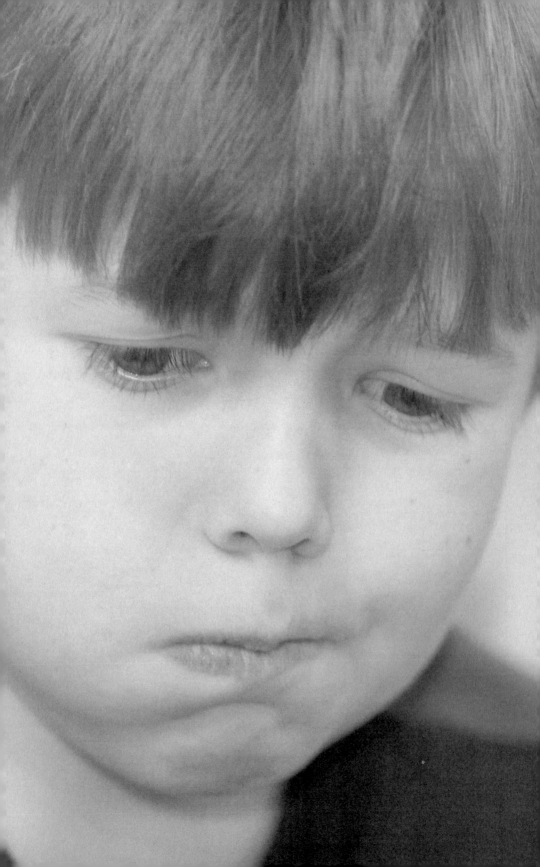

My Pain

It doesn't hurt with sudden screams
like cuts, or stings, or scrapes.
It doesn't help to cover it
with bandages and tapes.

It doesn't make me howl like
I'm waiting for a shot,
or when I touch my finger to
the stove when I should not.

It isn't like those frozen brains
you get some summer day
when ice cream burns behind your eyes
then quickly melts away.

It's more a steady soreness,
like a nasty, nagging blister.
If you have got a pain like mine,
it's probably your sister.

Funner

Broccoli's funner than spinach,
and french fries are funner than peas.
Pizza is funner than liver and onions,
and burgers are funner with cheese.

Waffles are funner than pancakes,
and hot dogs are funner than steak.
I bet you will agree with me
that ice cream is funner with cake.

Lemonade's funner in summer sun,
and cocoa is funner in snow.
And when you're opening presents,
faster is funner than slow.

Swimming is funner than homework,
and bathtubs are funner with boats.
And just about anything's funner
than writing thank you notes.

Dirty is funner than washing your ears,
and growing is funner than small.
And watching a bully get caught by a teacher
could be the funnest of all.

But surely the funnest thing in the world
is pretending you couldn't have heard,
when your mother tells you, again and again,
that "funner isn't a word."

Lost

I'm feeling lost,
my pain is deep.
I'll never get
a wink of sleep.

I'll stay completely
wide awake
until I find
my missing snake.

My mother,
I'm surprised to see,
is even more
concerned than me.

How To Ask For a Kitten

You want to get a kitten?
Or maybe even two?
Listen very closely,
I'll tell you what to do.

Your parents both will smile and say,
"A kitten? Why, of course!"
If you begin by telling them
you're dying for a horse.

Zooming to the Moon

I've built myself a spaceship
to zoom me to the moon.
If you would like to come along,
I'm leaving fairly soon.

We'll have to wait a week or two—
I hope you'll understand.
I'm waiting till the moon is full
so we'll have room to land.

Air and Space Museum

My private Air and Space Museum's
opening next week.
If you would like, I'll let you in
to have a little peek.

Just step inside this empty room—
please, go ahead and stare,
As you enjoy the lovely space
and breathe the awesome air.

My Father is a Baby

My father is a baby—
I wish it wasn't true.
I'm sure he is embarrassed but
there's nothing he can do.

He doesn't whine or whimper
or cry like babies can.
He may be just a baby,
but he takes it like a man.

You see, my Dad's a leap year kid
with every child's fears.
To celebrate his birthday
he has to wait four years.

The hardest thing for him, I'm sure,
is not that he must wait.
It's that his son (that's me) is nine,
while he is only eight.

TV Scream

I battle with my brother
each time we watch TV.
He tries to be the boss and say
the shows we're going to see.

But when a howling hurricane
comes roaring from my throat,
I'm guaranteed to always win
the fight for the remote.

Sweet Dream

Last night, I dreamed a chocolate rain
kersplattered from the sky.
It drizzled down vanilla snow
in mountains miles high.

As fudgy rivers bubbled past,
a breeze began to blow.
It sprinkled nuts and cherries on
the surface of the snow.

I grabbed a spoon to try a taste,
or maybe more than one.
But then my mother woke me up
and spoiled all my fun.

I wrestled with that dream all day—
it teased my hungry head.
When I got home from school I raced
and dove into my bed.

I know a dream is just a dream
but I'd be brokenhearted
if I did not go back there quick
and finish what I started.

The Perfect Gift for Mother's Day

The perfect gift
for Mother's Day—
and you don't have to buy it.

Give her what
she really wants—
a bunch of peace and quiet.

My Brother is a Zero

My brother is a zero—
a nothing, I'm afraid.
My mother keeps reminding me
it's just how he was made.

My brother's been a zero
at least a month or two.
The little slug is nothing but
a boring dream come true.

He never wants to listen,
or do the things I say.
He's lazy as a sleepy sloth
who hangs around all day.

At hide and seek, he's hopeless.
At kick the can, he's slow.
I ask him what he'd like to play?
The nothing doesn't know.

My brother's just a zero.
He simply isn't fun.
I'm hoping he'll be more alive
when he turns one.

You're Gonna Get It

You're gonna get it, any minute.
I smell trouble, and you are in it.

You're gonna get it, yessiree.
I'm glad it's you and isn't me.

You're gonna get it, soon and sore.
Like nothing you have got before.

You're gonna get it, wait and see.
I wish I knew what it's gonna be.

You're gonna get it, I'm gonna tell.
And giggle as you start to yell.

You're gonna get it, have no fear.
As soon as Mom and Dad get here.

You're gonna get it, say "GOODBYE!"

(I wish I could remember why.)

Morning Advice

I do not give
a lot of tips,
but take this
as a warning:

Steer clear of Dad
until he's had
his coffee
in the morning.

Gold Medal Kid

Two million eyes are watching me.
A million tongues are cheering.
The fears I might have felt before
are quickly disappearing.

Tonight I'm feeling ready—
completely on my game.
My nerves are cool as arctic ice.
I'm hotter than a flame.

I turn and twist, and float and fly,
as if my arms were wings.
I rise so high I touch the sky—
my legs are filled with springs.

I scoff and laugh at gravity,
defying all its laws.
With every leap, I hear the cheers
and thunderous applause.

Olympic dreams of glory
are soaring in my head.
For I'm the best that ever lived
at bouncing on my bed.

Driving Our Parents

(A Perfectly Delightful Car Poem
for Two Sweet Voices)

He's pinching my fingers!

She's pulling my hair!

He's laughing too loudly!

She's breathing my air!

He's touching my shoulder!

She's stomping my shoes!

He's punching my muscles!

She's bashing my bruise!

He's hearing my music!

She's smelling my snack!

He's stealing my answers!

She won't give them back!

He's watching my window!

Her knee's on my side!

He's making up stories!

I promise, she lied!

My brother's a doofus!

My sister's a freak!

We're driving to Grandma's

to stay for a week!

We're doing our best

to be absolute pains!

We're driving our parents

clear out of their brains!

Why?

Why is dirt so dirty?
And why is air so airy?
Why is soap so soapy?
And why are scares so scary?

Why is water so watery?
And why is cream so creamy?
Why is butter so buttery?
And why are dreams so dreamy?

Why is soup so soupy?
And why are burps so burpy?
Why is juice so juicy?
And why are slurps so slurpy?

Why are moms so Mommy?
And why is silk so silky?
Why are dads so Daddy?
And why is milk so milky?

Why are clouds so cloudy?
And why is sun so sunny?
Why are rhymes so rhymy?
And why is fun so funny?

Music Money

Danny and I play saxophone—
we started up last week.
We both can blow a note or two,
but mostly we just squeak.

Danny gets a dollar
for his playing, from his Pop.
My dad paid me double that,
to encourage me to stop.

Recycling is the Greatest

Recycling is the greatest thing
that each of us can do.
We send our plastic out, and then
it's back as something new!

It works for glass and paper too—
we trade them in for others.
I wonder if recycling works
for very bossy brothers?

I'm in Love

My heart is beating faster and
my palms are sort of sweaty.
My cheeks are blushing badly and
my knees are far from steady.

My brain is rollercoastering
as if I'm in a dream.
I get this way when I'm in love...
with chocolate ice cream.

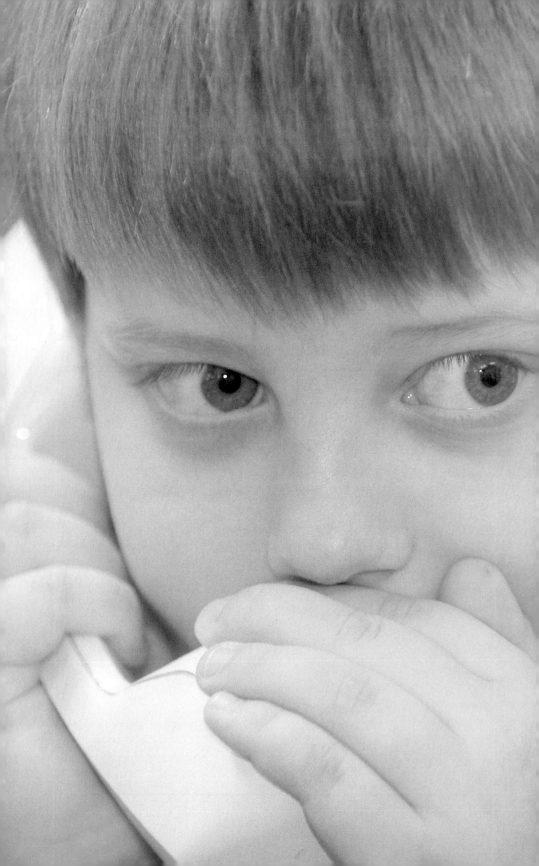

My Sister Said a Secret

My sister said a secret
and warned me not to share it.
But if I couldn't tell you now
I know I couldn't bear it.

My sister said to zip my lips
or she would make me cry.
But since you asked me for the truth
I simply shouldn't lie.

My sister said if someone hears
she'll say it isn't so.
But you are not just "someone"
so I think you should know.

She said, "Don't tell a single soul.
I'll punch you if you do!"
(I haven't told a single soul...
I just told Billy when he called,
and now I'm telling you.)

So that is not a single soul—
It's two!

A Mouth Full

Our dinner conversation
was dangerous last night.
My dad was mad, I guess,
because I took too big a bite.

And when I asked a question
with my cheeks all crammed with food,
I think he said my manners
were extremely rough and rude.

Although his eyes were fiery
and he snorted like a bull,
I couldn't understand him well—
his mouth was just too full.

How to Beat a Bully

I did it Dad. I didn't run.
I stayed and stood my ground
when, on my way to school today
a bully pushed me down.

I told him that I wasn't scared
and he was not so tough.
And if he wasn't careful
it could get a little rough.

He wanted me to fight him
but I told him you'd be mad.
And then I got a great idea—
I said you'd fight his dad!

I said that you were strong as steel
and ready to attack.
That you could beat his father
with a hand behind your back.

The bully and his father
will be here any minute.
My friends have come to watch the fight
and cheer you when you win it.

You *never* want to fight him, Dad?
I guess I sort of knew it.
It's not important anyway...

I'm sure that Mom will do it.

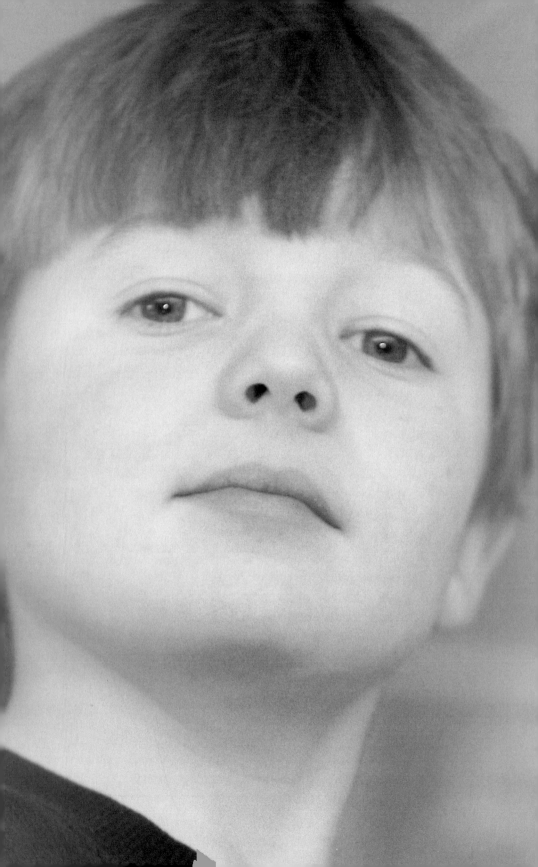

I Did It

Okay, it's true, I did it.
It's time that I confessed.
I thought I'd keep it to myself
but honesty is best.

It's time that I admitted it.
I feel I shouldn't lie.
It's difficult to say it but
I guess I'd better try.

What you're hearing from my lips
is positively true.
I cannot blame my brother like
I sometimes always do.

I need to be responsible
and say that it was me.
I cannot hide it anymore—
it's here for all to see.

I did it and I'm pretty proud.
Now you're the first to know it.
I promise you with all my heart
I am this poem's poet.

I Need to Scream

I need to scream—
it's so unfair.
I have to quickly
fill the air

With all the noise
my throat can blast—
long and loud,
and full and fast.

A screech so shrill
that people fly
to plug their ears
and cringe and cry.

A shriek as dark
and thick as mud
that instantly
will curdle blood.

The world will know
my howl, and fear it,
as soon as Mom
gets home to hear it.

Scream Quietly, Please

"If you scream, be quiet.
If you run, go slow.
Please be patient—stop and wait,
unless you need to go.
If you jump in mounds of mud,
please avoid the dirt.
If you fall and scrape your knee,
please do not get hurt.
If you play, please go outside,
but don't get too much sun.
Being silly's fine unless
you're having too much fun.
Feeling sad can be okay,
as long as you don't cry.
Answer all my questions please
but do not ask me why.
Be concerned a tiny bit,
but never, ever worry.
Take your time with homework,
but do it in a hurry.
It doesn't matter if you lose,
as long as you're the winner.
And if you lose your appetite,
be sure to eat your dinner."

These things my parents say to me
are not at all amusing.
They think my life is laughs and fun,
but, mostly, it's confusing.

My Birthday Was a Blast

My birthday was
a blast this year—
we all had so much fun
that, next year,
I've decided
to have another one!

The Man
Who Named
the Funny Bone

The man who named
the funny bone
I sadly should explain
had buckets full of gravy where
he should have had a brain.

I know he was a phony
who loved to be confusing,
'cause I just hit that bone again,
and it was not amusing.

Dads Are Great

Dads are great
for tons of things—
too many
to express.

Best of all
when Mom says "No!"
Dads are great
for "Yes!"

I'd Better Get in Trouble Now

Right now
I'm just a boy.
Soon
I'll be a man.

I guess I'd better
get in trouble
now,
while I can.

A Pressing Question

Mom,
answer my question
please:
If potatoes
taste better
piled and pushed,
squeezed and smooshed,
glopped and smashed,
and plopped and mashed,
then
why not peas?

Waiting Waiting Waiting

We're
waiting
waiting
waiting
for the
doctor
doctor
doctor
and my
mother
mother
mother's
mad as ice.

Since I'm
waiting
waiting
waiting
for a
shot
shot
shot,
all this
waiting
waiting
waiting's
very nice.

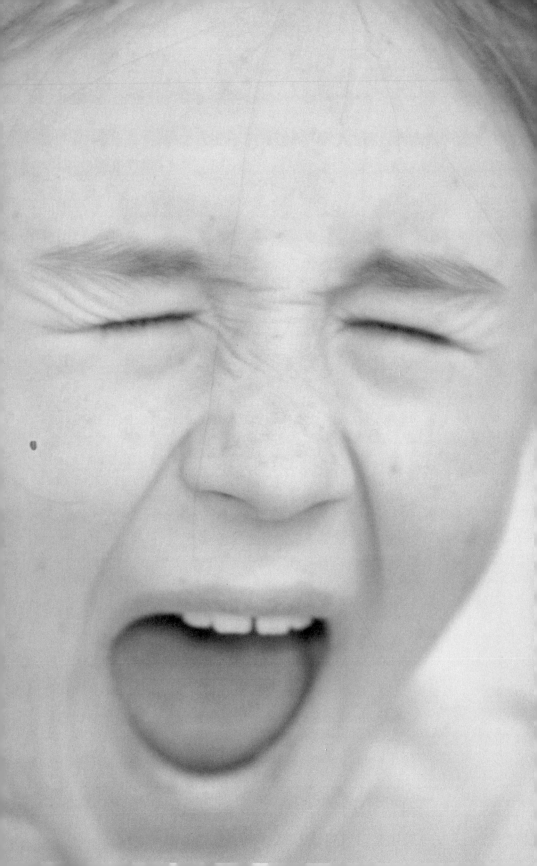

Sore Head

Mom is mad at Daddy,
and Dad is mad at Mommy.
I'm sandwiched in between them
like a slice of sad salami.

When everyone is snarling
and anger's in the air,
it's not a super time to have
your mother brush your hair.

Worst Nightmare Ever

Wake up Mommy, right away!
You have to help me, Dad!
I've had a scare and need to share
the nightmare I just had!

Crabs were crawling in my bed
to tickle all my toes.
And bats were zooming 'round my head
and landing on my nose.

A family of wiggle worms
were nesting in my hair.
And very smelly jelly fish
were oozing up my chair.

Monsters creaking on the stairs
were rumbling and groaning.
Principals in swivel chairs
were grumbling and phoning.

Snakes were squirming on my floor
and wrapping all around me.
Bullies pounded on my door
and laughed because they'd found me.

They made me eat a dozen rotten
old and moldy eggs.
And I have not forgotten all
those spiders on my legs.

But none of this was really bad
compared to what came last.
I had to wake you, Mom and Dad,
and do it really fast.

Nothing that I saw tonight
was quite as bad as this is...

I dreamed Aunt Alice hugged me tight,
and slobbered me with kisses!

Why Is the Bathroom Mirror So High?

I see the top of my head today.
It's looking pretty good.

I'd love to see the rest of me...
In five more years, I should.

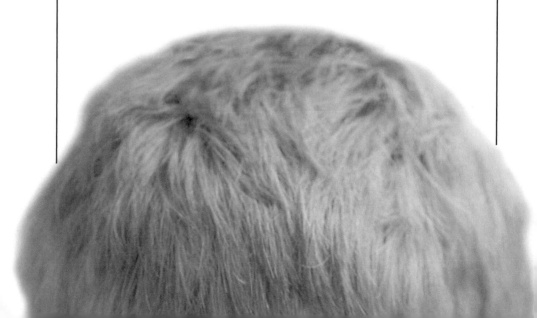

A VERY, VERY Important
Message for Mom

I love when you come
to my games and cheer.
But let me make one thing
perfectly clear:

It's great when you hoot,
and you holler, and scream.
But PLEASE!
PLEASE!
don't ever shout,
    "Go Sweetie!
    "Go Honey!"
    "Go Cutie!"
    "Go Baby!"
    "Go Dearie!"
    "Go Darling!"
and especially
    "Go Buttercup!"
in front of my team.

At The Beep...

"How you doing, Grandpa?
I am doing great!
I have so much to tell you
I can hardly barely wait!

I got an A in math today,
and reading's really fun.
We played a kickball game at Gym
and my team won!

Mom's away on business,
and Dad is wicked stressed.
The dog just ate my slippers,
and my brother is a pest.

That's the news from here today,
I hope you're doing fine.
We're going out to dinner now—
we should be back by nine.

Call us back on OUR machine;
that would be super sweet...
And someday, maybe, you and I,
may really even MEET!"

The Momster

I have a Momster in my house
who's strong and sometimes scary.
She's twice as huggy as my Dad,
but only half as hairy.

Her arms can wrap around you fast,
like solid bands of steel.
She doesn't seem to care at all
how kids like me can feel.

The Momster loves to hug you tight,
and kiss you on your cheek.
She'll do it even harder if
you whimper, whine or shriek.

It doesn't matter when or where—
the Momster will attack.
In front of all my friends, I'll get
a sudden smoochy smack.

To get a kiss like this from her
is always a disaster.
There's nothing in this kissy world
that makes my feet move faster.

So, when I hear the Momster's near,
I race to run and hide.
But she can always sniff me out,
or in, if I'm inside.

Like now, I hear her clicking
up the stairs and down the hall.
And now, I see her shadow
like a giant on my wall.

I can't escape the Momster now.
I'm trapped inside my bed.
Perhaps she'll go away if I
pretend that I am dead.

Too late! Her claws are closing like
the pinchers on a bug!
And now the Momster's giving me
a mother-Momster hug!

Aaaaaaaaa!

Three Words

I heard three words from Dad today
I didn't expect to hear.
They jumped like jackrabbits out of his mouth
and raced around my ears.

A look of panic crossed his face
and danced inside his eyes.
I didn't try to hide from him
my smile of surprise.

I hugged him tight and told him,
"You only said what's true.
I knew one day I'd hear those words,
and, Dad, 'I love you' too!"

Just Once

Just once
I'd love to leave for school
and leave my room a mess.
And maybe do a "NO" or two
instead of always "YES."

Just once
I'd love to linger in
a dreamy steamy shower.
I'd stay a couple days or weeks,
or even just an hour.

Just once
I'd love to stay up late
to see what's on TV.
And race outside at midnight
and climb my favorite tree.

Just once
I'd love to pick and lick
a monster ice cream cone.
Then buy a truck of candy bars
and eat them all alone.

Just once
I might discover that,
although these things are nice,
they'd be a whole lot better if
I did them all
just twice.

Dirty Words

I learned some dirty words today
while spying on my dad.
As he was digging in our yard
he got a little mad.

With every single shovel full
he used a different word.
I couldn't quite believe my ears
were hearing what they heard.

I stayed as still as midnight
so, my father never caught me.
And now, I bet, you'd like to hear
the dirty words he taught me.

His words flew out as quickly as
a wild waterfall.
I may have left a couple out
but here's what I recall:

"Filthy, yucky,
foul, mucky,
smelly, sticky,
vile, icky,
sludgy, muddy,
grungy, cruddy,
wormy, musty,
smirchy, dusty,
dumpy, gloppy,
sooty, sloppy,
snotty, slimy,
gross and grimy,
grubby, slushy,
marshy, mushy,
swampy, danky,
reeky, ranky,
putrid," and I've not forgotten
"moldy" and
a little "rotten."

I know these words are hard to hear
so I will not repeat them.
But now you know some dirty words
if you should ever need them.

My Mom Forgot

I can't believe my mom forgot
to make my bed today.
I don't remember when she hasn't
put my clothes away.

I washed my face all by myself,
and even cleaned my ears.
She hasn't missed a chance to scrub
in sixty thousand years.

She wasn't there to tell me
all the stuff I need to wear.
And, for the first time ever
she forgot to brush my hair.

She didn't fix my breakfast
or make my lunch and snack.
I even had to wash and put
my dishes in the rack.

She didn't pack my bookbag
or make her normal fuss.
Without her silly questions
I was early for the bus.

I haven't got the slightest clue
how Mom got so off track.
But I can tell you, here and now,
I want my old Mom back!

It's Not Because

It's not because you told me to
I'll clean my bedroom floor.
It's not because you want me to
I'll close the bathroom door.

It's not because you like things neat
I'm picking up my toys.
It's not because you yelled at me
I'm turning off my noise.

It's not because you said it
for the million billionth time,
I'll take my stinky sneakers out
and scrape away the slime.

I'll even wash my face and hands,
and button up my shirt.
I do this stuff for ME, you know...
(because I want dessert.)

Stuff Box

I found a cool box
to put stuff in.
It's not too deep
and not too thin.

It's not too narrow
not too wide.
My stuff will love
being stuffed inside.

It's not too heavy
not too light—
the perfect place for all my stuff
to fall asleep at night.

I'm going to start to use this box
in just another minute.
But first I need to look around
for stuff to put in it.

Candy Ache

I gobbled twenty chocolate bars
'cause my mother said I shouldn't.
I licked a hundred lollipops
'cause my brother bet I couldn't.

Fifty squishy licorice sticks
were calling and I knew it.
I ate them all with bubble gum
to see if I could do it.

I gulped a dozen peanut cups—
I knew it might be bad to.
But all of it was urging me
to eat it, so I had to.

Don't tell a soul I said this
or I'll never be your friend,
but I never want to see
another candy bar again.

(Until tomorrow.)

Brothers' Day

Let's all celebrate
Brothers' Day
some dreary night
in early May.

We'll whoop and cheer—
oh, yes, we won't.
A day for brothers,
and all they don't.

We'll give them gifts—
the best we couldn't.
Sing them songs—
the ones we shouldn't.

Sprinkle ants
between their sheets.
Bake them
spinach cake with beets.

Slip some worms
inside their snacks.
Slap a sign
across their backs.

Knot the laces
of each shoe.
Squeeze in
globs of super glue.

Order extra
vaccinations.
Sent them all
on long vacations.

So, Hip! Hip! Hooray for Brothers' Day!
I'll cheer until I'm blue!
Hey, wait... I just remembered...
I'm a brother too.

(Are you a sister?
Here's an ending for you.
Just change the last two
lines to read:)
"I'll work to make my brother's day
a sister's dream come true.")

Shopping on TV is So Easy!

We're getting a "Super Juicer"—
I ordered it today.
And we'll be cooking chicken soon
"The New and Modern Way."

I also got a "Fast 'n Easy
Pasta Maker" too.
I didn't buy the "Smoker" though—
'cause smoking's bad for you.

They're sending me a "Wonder Knife"
that sliced a metal bar!
And, yesterday, I bought my Dad
some "Magic in a Jar!"

Just in time for Mother's Day
I got a diamond ring!
I know you won't believe me
but they didn't cost a thing!

The TV gave the number—
I grabbed the phone and dialed.
They make it very easy—
even for a child.

They didn't ask for money.
I guess they never will.
To share their "thanks" they said, instead
they're sending Dad a bill!

Nasty Names

When I use a nasty name
I always get in trouble.
I called my brother two of them
and got in trouble double.

So I invented special names
that I can use instead.
My brother made me mad today
and this is what I said:

"You
Stink-o-matic! Pudding Head!
Rumbledumper! Soggy Bed!
Ear Wax Eater! Pickle Pox!
Barfer Belly! Smelly Socks!
Potty Snotter! Doodledork!
Scummy gumball on a fork!
Rotten Cauliflower Face!
Dunderbum from Outer Space!
Fuddlenutter! Boo-Boo-Brain!
Boogerbreath! And Toilet Train!"

I didn't think they sounded bad
especially from a kid.
But I am missing dinner now
because my mother did.

The Moon is a Pizza

The moon is a pizza
tonight in the sky.
It's calling me closer—
my hunger is high.

It's just how I love it—
a sausagy sight,
with fresh mozzarella
all oozy and white.

Let's fly up and grab it—
but, if you don't mind,
I'm planning to leave
all the mushrooms behind.

There's Nothing
Quite as Frightening

Tonight a very scary show
appeared on our TV.
I dove into some pillows so
I couldn't hear or see.

Without a gun, or monster,
or beasts from outer space,
the sights I sneaked a peek to see
brought terror to my face.

Although no thirsty vampires slurped,
no zombies took a bite,
I never hope to see again
the things I saw tonight.

My sister wasn't happy with
my screams, and boos, and hissing,
but there's nothing quite as frightening as
a couple people kissing.

My Two Stomachs

My mother won't believe me but
I'm pretty sure it's true—
most kids have one stomach,
but I was born with two.

The first is just for normal food—
potatoes, salad, meat.
It fills up very rapidly
at dinner when we eat.

When Stomach One is full and fat
it knows just what to do.
It tells my brain to open up
the doors of Stomach Two.

I tell my mom that, "One is done.
It has a stomach ache.
But Stomach Two is open wide
and ready for some cake."

Diet Quiet

Learn to be quiet
when Dad's on a diet.
The best thing to do
is shut up and chew.

If you must be a pest
then let me suggest
you wait till after dinner
to say he isn't thinner.

Sunday Funnies

My dad just read the comics
in the Sunday News Gazette.
He laughed so hard he spilled his milk
and hasn't stopped yet.

He passed the funnies on to Mom
who howled to her toes.
The coffee she was sipping shot
like rockets out her nose.

My older sister grabbed them
and although she tried to fight it
her giggles zoomed around the room
like bombs had been ignited.

I pulled the paper from her hand
as laughter just increased...

Funny?
I don't find
these funnies funny
in the **least**.

I Can't Make Up My Mind

Oh, I don't know. It's just too hard.
I can't make up my mind.
This is the worst! Can you go first?
I need some extra time.

It's like a test. I'm feeling stressed
by all these anxious voices.
Would everybody please hush up
so I can make my choices?

I feel like I am being squeezed.
The pressure's just too great.
But if I don't decide right now
my future may not wait.

My brain is feeling frozen like
it's in a chilly trance.
But if I take too long I might
not get a second chance.

I'm feeling lost and so confused.
I'd like to phone a friend.
I wish I knew just when
this awful agony will end.

The time has finally come, I fear,
I'm in the danger zone.
Okay......

    two scoops
    of chocolate, please.
    And on a sugar cone.

Scooter Blues

I think I've got some broken bones
but they're not broke too bad.
I'm never sure of all the bumps
my dizzy head has had.

My knees are scraped and drippy.
My wrists are sprained and sore.
I've ripped my pants a dozen times
and torn my jacket four.

My shoes are held together with
some sticky silver tape.
My body's bruised so black and blue
I'm looking like a grape.

I secretly would love to be
at home on my computer.
But I'll pretend for all my friends
I love this silly scooter.

"Room to Grow"

I cannot find my fingers,
I'll never touch a toe,
because my parents always buy
my clothes with
"room to grow."

My saggy pants are dragging like
a tortoise in the snow
since everyone decided
I needed
"room to grow."

My shrimpy feet are swimming,
my run is sad and slow,
because my socks and shoes have got
some extra
"room to grow."

And way up high, above my eyes,
a final, crowning blow—
They've cut my hair so short I'm bald,
so it has, (you guessed it)
"room to grow."

Dynamite Driver

My dad's a dynamite driver
as all the neighbors know.
He gets explosive easily
and lets his anger show.

When dad gets mad, he waves and shouts
and shares a lot of stress.
He says some things I can't repeat,
so you'll just have to guess.

He tells me not to listen
but I do it anyway.
So now when we go driving
I know just what to say.

Just like Dad, I've now become
a raving, screeching creature...

"Hey you!"
"Get lost!"
"Stay off the road!"

Uh oh.
That was my *teacher*.

I'm Sinking

Throw me a lifeline.
I'm sinking in stuff.
I'm drowning in toys.
The ocean is rough.

My homework's gone under.
I can't find my clothes.
It's getting so murky,
I can't see my toes.

My bed was right here
just a moment ago.
Now it's gone, and just where
I will sleep, I don't know.

Launch all the lifeboats!
Disaster is nearing!
The water is rising!
My room's disappearing!

I don't mean to scare you
with all of this noise,
and tidal wave mountains
of toppling toys,

So jump while you can, and
start swimming away.
I know it sounds crazy,
but I want to stay.

As I bravely go down
with my ship I'll confess,
in spite of the dangers...

I LOVE A GOOD MESS.

Sleep Tricks

I zoomed around all day
and now I'm ready for my bed.
My body tells me "nighty night,"
but what about my head?

My brain won't let me go to sleep.
It's screaming, "Stay Awake!"
My mind is racing down a hill
and, guess what? There's no brake!

I'm trying every trick I know
to end this wild ride.
I've looked around for sheep to count
but they all run and hide.

I think I've found the answer to
my problem for tonight.
I'll get to dreamland faster if
I just turn off my light.

It's working! Now I'm yawning and
the fog is getting deep.
Now if I take my headphones off
I might just fall asleep.

Zac

Spencer

Dominique

Austin

Maya

William

John

Jane

Clayton

Annie

Ben

Peter

Whit

**Thanks
to the
Crew!**

Ted Scheu

Ted Scheu (rhymes with "That Poetry Guy") is a widely-published author of poems for kids. His work has appeared in numerous poetry anthologies in the US (Philomel and Meadowbrook Press) and in the UK (Macmillan, Scholastic, and Hodder Children's Books), and in his collections "I Tickled My Teachers" and "I Threw My Brother Out."

When he isn't writing, or playing outdoors with his family, Ted (a former elementary teacher) can be found bounding around the world to schools, inspiring kids (like you!) to find their own writers' voices. You can learn more about Ted, his books, poems, and school programs at his web site: **www.poetryguy.com**. Ted lives with his family in Middlebury, Vermont.

Peter Lourie

Peter Lourie is an explorer-adventurer, anthropologist, canoeist, photographer, and teacher, as well as author. His books have won numerous awards, including the International Eco Award for Excellence from the Natural Resources Defense Council. Peter has explored and written books about many of the most remote and rugged regions and rivers of the world including the Amazon, the Everglades, the Missouri, the Rio Grande, the Hudson, and the Erie Canal. His "River Series," for readers age 9 and up, is published by Boyds Mills Press. You can learn much more about Peter at his web site **www.peterlourie.com**.

In gracious support of this project, Peter plopped down his pen and paddle, and picked up his camera to capture these remarkable faces. Peter lives with his family in Weybridge, Vermont.

Winslow Colwell

Winslow Colwell is a marvelously-multi-talented designer of books, kites, and all things printable—many of which can be found at his web site at **www.wcolwell.com**. He lives with his family in Ripton, Vermont.

Need more copies of "I Froze My Mother" for your favorite 1,000 friends and relatives?

1. For super-speedy delivery, go to Ted's web site at **www.poetryguy.com** and push the "Order Books!" link, and you will be zoomed right to the publisher.

2. Fly over to Ted's web site at **www.poetryguy.com**, print out an order form, then snail-mail it to Ted. If you order directly from Ted, he can sign the books for you. Please let him know exactly how you'd like him to inscribe them, when you order.

You may also just send a check by mail for $12.95 (US$) for each book to Ted Scheu, PO Box 564, Middlebury, VT 05753, USA. Please include $3.00 (US) for postage and handling for up to four books, and $3.00 for each four books after that. To order from outside the US, go to #1 above.

3. Or you can surf right over to **amazon.com**, or **barnesandnoble.com**, or **borders.com** and order the book there.

4. Politely ask your wonderful local bookstore order the book for you.

Thanks!